relationships 101™

girls:
being best
friends

Diane Bailey

rosen publishing's
rosen
central®

New York

Published in 2013 by The Rosen Publishing Group, Inc.
29 East 21st Street, New York, NY 10010

First Edition

Library of Congress Cataloging-in-Publication Data

Bailey, Diane, 1966–
Girls:being best friends/Diane Bailey. — 1st ed.
     p. cm. —(Relationships 101)
Includes bibliographical references and index.
ISBN 978-1-4488-6831-5 (library binding) —
ISBN 978-1-4488-6834-6 (pbk.) —
ISBN 978-1-4488-6838-4 (6-pack)
1. Friendship in adolescence–Juvenile literature. 2. Female friendship–Juvenile literature. 3. Best friends–Juvenile literature. I. Title.
BF724.3.F64B35 2013
158.2'5–dc23

                                                                    2012003285

Manufactured in the United States of America

CPSIA Compliance Information: Batch #S12YA: For further information, contact Rosen Publishing, New York, New York, at 1-800-237-9932.

CONTENTS

20

26

introduction

She's the popular girl, the one who always has a whole group of girls to eat lunch with and another whole group wanting to be her partner for a history project. Will you find her home on Friday night or sitting by herself at a football game? Not likely. It's more likely you'd need a guide to help fight your way through the group of girls stuck to her. But who are all those people surrounding her? There's a difference between being popular and having friends— real friends.

There's nothing wrong with being popular. Some people are just like that. They're fun and charismatic, and they naturally draw people to them. They might genuinely like having a lot of people around, all the time. As long as some of those people are true friends, that's fine. Other people are quieter. They want only a few friends. Either way is ok.

Having someone to hang out with is a big part of friendship. But it's not the only thing that matters. Good friends offer each other a lot more. A true friend is both someone you like and someone you trust. It's a girl who not only answers the phone when you call but also takes the time to listen to what you have to say. If you're happy about something, she's going to be happy with you. If you're unhappy or worried, she'll help you figure out what to do. And if you put your heads together and still can't figure out what to do, then she'll just sympathize.

A real friend likes you for who you really are. Let's face it: all of us have things about us that are, well, a little weird. A true friend doesn't care. In fact, those may be the things she likes best of all.

CHAPTER ONE

GETTING OUT THERE

There is one rule about friendship: everybody needs at least one. Beyond that, however, things get fuzzy. Friendships are personal. They are like a contract between two people, and only those two people have the power to set the "rules" within that particular friendship.

People are complicated creatures. They all have a unique set of things that makes them who they are. It's a combination of the things they like to do, their personality traits, their past experiences, and their dreams for the future. It's no surprise people make friends for different reasons and on different levels.

The Family You Choose

There's a common saying that goes, "You can't choose your family." There's another

At school, at a sleepover, or at a beach party, best friends make the good things even more enjoyable and the hard things a little easier to deal with.

saying, too: "Friends are the family you choose." A person's family is made up of people who will always be there for her, in good times and bad, no matter what. That's what good friends are like, too.

It's tempting to think that the more friends someone has, the better. If one friend is absent from school or busy on Saturday, there are plenty more to fall back on. More friends mean more options, right? Well, yes. And no.

The best approach is probably somewhere in the middle. Having dozens of friends will likely make it difficult to keep up with everyone. There simply isn't enough time in the day to catch up with what's going on in their lives, much less have any kind of deeper conversation. On the other hand, having only one good friend, or even two, limits flexibility. If you're always hanging out with the same girl, you or she (or both of you) could end up getting tired of each other. That doesn't mean one of you is a bad friend or a boring person—it simply means that everyone needs a chance to expand her horizons.

People choose friends for different reasons. They might bond over a common interest, like playing the guitar or competing on the track team, and want someone with whom they can share the experience. They might get to know each other simply because they are thrust into the same circumstances, whether it's being lab partners in science or because they always run into each other when they're out walking their dogs.

That first connection can come from anything—whether it's sports or school or Scouts. After that, however, it's important to evaluate the reasons to stay in a friendship. Good friends genuinely care about each other's feelings. They don't make each other feel bad about being themselves or try to pressure the other into becoming someone else. Friends don't have to spend every minute in each other's company, but when they are together, it's time they both enjoy.

Meeting People

If you've lived in the same town for several years, you may already have an established group of friends. But if you've moved or switched schools, you may be separated from your old group. Or, as you get older, it may be that your personality and priorities are changing. You may want to make new friends who are more in tune with the person you are becoming.

Some friendships just kind of "happen"—two people meet each other, hit it off, and become friends. Obviously, a friendship won't work if there's no chemistry or common ground. But sometimes it's hard

Being in a new town or at a new school often brings feelings of loneliness and being an outsider, but finding a new group of friends can mean new opportunities.

to meet people in the first place. This can be especially challenging for people who are in a new school or town, or for people who are shy. Meeting people can feel intimidating—there's no question about that. However, most people are friendly, and they're probably curious about the "new girl," too.

It's OK to start small. If you're in the same class with someone, talking about a project is a natural way to start up a conversation. Next, look around for activities you might like to do. Audition for the school play, join the orchestra, or volunteer at the animal shelter. This is a great way to find people who share similar interests, and you won't have to figure out something to talk about.

With the Internet, it's easy to meet people online—through forums for groups or even as "friends of friends" through social networking sites like

LONG-DISTANCE FRIENDSHIPS

You may not get to have a sleepover every weekend, but long-distance friendships can be fun, too. Perhaps you have a pen pal (or e-mail pal) who lives in a different part of the country or even another country altogether. If you are writing back and forth, it's not as important for your personalities to "click" because you're not spending actual time together. However, having these friends can be a great way to connect with someone who shares a similar interest or can introduce you to something new.

Facebook. However, although the online world opens up doors to all kinds of people, meeting them in person should be approached very carefully. People can pretend to be anyone they want online, and that's not necessarily who they are in real life. If you've met someone online and now want to meet her in person, check with your parents and have one of them, or another adult, go with you. Do not go alone.

Most important, show that you are open to making friends. Smile at people to let them know you are approachable. Also, remember that the first impression you make of someone might not be the most accurate. People have lots of layers. Someone who seems unfriendly may just be shy. Someone who is loud or obnoxious might just be trying to cover up her insecurities. Give people a chance and save your judgment until you know them a little better. Friends don't have to be exactly alike. In fact, you might find that some of your best friends are those people who look at the world a little differently than you do.

Being Friends with a Boy

In elementary school, girls don't usually have that much in common with boys. The boys stay at their tables in the cafeteria, and the girls stay at theirs. They might talk a little bit for school, but otherwise, no thanks! However, when girls get older and enter middle school, that starts to change. They find out that boys are people, too. Boys may act differently, but that doesn't automatically make them aliens or even bad friends. They're just different.

Girls who have brothers or have had a chance to be around a friend's brother may

Guy friends can be valuable — they offer a whole different perspective on life that maybe your girl friends don't have. They understand what it's like to be a guy!

already be used to boys and have friends who are guys. Some girls prefer to have boys as friends because they tend to have less of the drama that can go along with girl friendships. Boys don't spend as much time gossiping. They don't seem to care as much about organizing or ranking their friendships and keeping tabs on who likes whom best. Instead, they're happy just hanging out. This can take a lot of pressure out of a relationship.

Of course, there can be pitfalls in boy-girl friendships. One person may start to like the other in a romantic way. If the other one doesn't return those feelings, that can make things awkward, to say the least. Even if they both feel that way, there's the chance that things won't work out in the long run. Then there's a different kind of awkwardness, as they have to figure out whether they can salvage a friendship out of a fizzled romance. In addition, friends of different genders may get hassled by their other friends. They might get teased about dating each other when that's not the case. And the more they insist they're just friends, the more they get teased. True friends, however, don't have to defend their choice of friends to other people. If they both enjoy each other's company, that's all that matters.

CHAPTER TWO

STAYING POWER

A checklist for friendship might include things like "similar interests" or "fun to be with." Hopefully, it would also include things like "trust" and "respect." People who take their friends for granted or treat them badly usually lose those friends in the long run. A friendship shouldn't feel like hard work all the time, but if the friendship is worth having in the first place, then it's worth putting in some effort.

The good news is, a lot of the energy that goes into building and maintaining a friendship is fun. It's about talking and laughing, spending time together, and sharing secrets. True friends will care about each other enough to weather the tough times and get back to the good ones.

Giving and Getting

Just as a plant will die if it doesn't get water, so will a

friendship. In this case, the "water" comes with a lot of ingredients, such as time and attention. A person who rarely spends any time with a friend should not realistically expect that person to be available. Friends have to show appreciation for the fact that they're there for each other and cultivate the relationship by doing things together.

Relationships are two-way streets. People don't want to feel as if they are the ones doing all the work in a relationship. They don't want to feel as if they value their friends more than they are valued themselves. Both people have to put in some time and effort to reassure the other person that she is a welcome and important part of the friendship.

Maintaining a friendship is like making a deal, or a series of deals: each person offers the other something in exchange for what she receives. It's not always an even trade, of course—that's the nature of friendship. For example, a girl whose parents are getting divorced may spend a lot of time at her friend's house, crying on her bed and eating up all her ice cream. She may completely ignore her friend's problems for a while. However, once she's gotten through this crisis, the friendship will likely be stronger. She will appreciate the support her friend gave her, and when the tables are turned and her friend is the one with problems, she'll be willing to return the favor.

On the other hand, it's dangerous to "overwater" a friendship. Spending time together is one thing, but spending too much time can actually damage a friendship. Adolescents are still growing into the people they will become as adults. This means experimenting with different activities and even different people.

Branching out does not mean you are shortchanging your friends. In fact, the things you do with other people can help enrich the friendships you already have. Whether it's learning to hang glide or simply finding an undiscovered hangout, you'll have new things to talk about with your old friends.

Competition and Jealousy

In middle school, girls often find themselves competing with each other. They want to be the prettiest, or have the nicest clothes, or get the cutest guy. That's a natural feeling, but it can be toxic to a friendship. At the root of friendship is the idea that two people like each other for who they are. One doesn't have to be the best at everything to earn the other person's acceptance. Likewise, a true friend will appreciate and celebrate the best qualities of

Competition and jealousy can ruin a good friendship. When the focus becomes about who is "better," it can erode the bond between two people.

her friend and not get jealous of her. A little competition can be fun, but too much can ruin a friendship. A person who is always trying to be the best at everything—or worse, trying to make her friends feel bad because of it—is missing the whole point of being a friend.

If you've ever found yourself feeling jealous of a friend, take a moment to figure out why. Is your friend flaunting her success and trying to make you feel bad? Is she telling you that you're not good enough? Or is it simply that you wish you were more like her? If it's the last one, then remind yourself that you are each your own person and that part of your responsibility in a friendship is to support her in the things that make her happy.

Sometimes the problem isn't about who is better at science or who got a better time in the 5K run. Another problem is when two of your friends don't like each other. This can put you in a tough spot because it might seem as if they are competing for you. Whenever you spend time with one, the other feels left out and gets angry or hurt. You can try to find something that all three of you might enjoy doing together and that would bring you closer together. However, don't feel that it's your job to make your friends like each other.

You're allowed to have different friends, and there's no requirement that says they have to get along, too.

How to Be a Good Friend

A lot of what goes into being a good friend is easy. You probably already want to spend time together, doing homework, going to the movies, or having sleepovers. Those are perfect, low-pressure times to talk about

GOSSIP

Girls talk. That's a fact. Sharing news about other people with your girlfriends is a way to feel connected. Knowing what people are doing, and what other people think about it, helps contribute to your own ideals of how to behave. But problems arise when the information being shared is hurtful or even false. Sometimes people who gossip are bonding by excluding someone else, and that's where things go wrong. Talking about people is one thing, but there's nothing good in taking pleasure from hurting or ostracizing someone else. Unfortunately, people who gossip may not even be saying what they really think because they're just trying to fit in.

school, family, or boys. And talking with your friends makes you feel better because it reassures you that you're not alone. The things you worry about are probably the same things your friends worry about. And it's nice to know there's someone who understands and is looking out for you. If you want to create a lasting friendship, here are some things to keep in mind:

- Be honest about what you think and what you want out of a friendship. If you don't think of a girl as your best friend, don't pretend that you do.
- Listen to what your friend has to say and consider her point of view. Even if you don't agree, she has a right to her own opinion.
- Be supportive of what she wants, whether it's a spot on the cheerleading squad or a long chat because she's depressed about something.

- Don't betray a friend by sharing her secrets or saying mean things about her.
- Respect her boundaries if she needs to keep something private or if she needs a little time to herself.
- Make time to nurture the friendship by spending time together. Have fun with activities you know you both love to do, and make a point to try new things as well.
- Forgive and forget when she hurts your feelings. Everybody makes mistakes, and if she's truly sorry, then holding a grudge will only make things worse.

Different Expectations

Even when two friends really get along, sometimes that's not enough. Different people want different things, and sometimes those things simply won't work together. It's not always easy to realize what's happening, but if

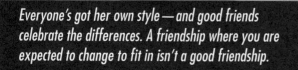

Everyone's got her own style — and good friends celebrate the differences. A friendship where you are expected to change to fit in isn't a good friendship.

you find that you're constantly disagreeing with a friend or feeling tense or uncomfortable with her, then the problem may be that you are not giving each other what you need. Maybe she wants to sit together at lunch every day, but you like to switch it up. Maybe she's totally into shopping, and you'd rather go camping.

See if you can talk about your different expectations. Before you do, remind yourself to keep in check any feelings of hurt or anger. It's OK to acknowledge these feelings, but don't let them rule you. The goal is to work things out, and if you let your emotions take over, it's going to be a lot harder.

Most friends have problems with each other from time to time. It goes with the territory of being close to someone. After all, if you barely knew one another, you wouldn't expect much from the other, and you wouldn't have anything to fight about. The trick is being able to communicate what you want, listen to your friend about what she wants, and then find a solution that will make you both happy.

CHAPTER THREE

TOUGH TIMES

When people feel angry or hurt, there's a reason. It's the brain's way of saying that something is wrong. That feeling could be justified. Or it could stem from a misunderstanding. But no matter where it comes from and why, the feeling itself is real, and it's a good idea to deal with it.

Fighting

Conflicts between friends are inevitable. No two people are the same, and even those who get along most of the time are bound to clash at some point. Disagreements don't have to be a terrible thing. In fact, sometimes they help two people see another side of an

> Even the best of pals don't see eye to eye all the time, but in a solid friendship, disagreements don't have to lead to arguing or fighting.

issue. However, if feelings of anger take over, then disagreements can spin out of control and turn into fights. Unfortunately, people in a fight are often more concerned with proving a point instead of trying to resolve the issue. They may want to hurt the other person with mean comments. Not surprisingly, fights don't usually accomplish much. They only make everyone feel worse.

Part of managing a friendship is learning when to "agree to disagree." Minor disagreements or differences of opinion aren't worth getting in a fight over, especially if there aren't other, bigger problems. Constantly calling people out over little things shows a lack of patience and tolerance. In general, arguments are valid when they relate to how people treat each other—not when they turn into heated discussions over a particular hairstyle. When friends do find themselves bickering—or even battling—over small stuff, it could be a sign of deeper problems in a relationship.

Talking It Out

Fighting is unpleasant and not usually productive. However, that does not mean you should ignore your feelings, or your friend's feelings, if one of you believes things aren't going well. The first step is to calm down. Next, pinpoint exactly what your friend did that made you angry. Consider why she acted that way—remember, there are two sides to every story. Now, figure out what changes need to occur to make you feel better. After you've thought through the problem rationally, talk to your friend. Pick a good time to do this. Don't just spring it on her when she's busy with something else.

WHAT'S HE DOING HERE?

Even the strongest friendships can hit some bumps in the road, and often those bumps are male. If one of you has a boyfriend and the other does not, it can cause some awkward moments. You may find yourself taking your boyfriend along whenever you and your girlfriend have plans. You may suffer from a case of "Friend Ditching Syndrome" and ignore her to spend time with him. Or, you may find that you are the one who gets bumped to second place. Even when one of you has a boyfriend, make a point to spend some time when it's just the two of you. And don't drop your friend for your new romance—if it ends, you'll need her more than ever.

Make sure each of you gets a chance to talk, and when it's your turn to listen, be sure you really do. There may be a good reason for her behavior, or she may not have realized what she did was hurtful. This is the time to collect information, not point fingers. Also, avoid making mean statements that are hard to take back.

Once you've each had your say, the next step is to find a solution. If you're lucky, it might be something easy. However, complicated problems may require you to compromise. If you do reach a compromise, remember that it's not about simply agreeing to something that moment. To make it work, you have to follow through on your part, even if it's not exactly what you wanted.

Also, don't be slow to apologize. Everyone makes mistakes. If you can admit them and show sincere regret for what you've done, then you're on the right track. But if you constantly insist that you're right or refuse to acknowledge where you messed up, people are likely going to get tired of your attitude. Also, learn to accept an apology gracefully. Don't gloat over the fact that you were right or try to punish someone even more by making her beg for your forgiveness.

When Friendships End

Perhaps you've had a best friend since third grade—or even before. Or maybe you have a circle of several friends whom you hang out with depending on your mood or what you're doing. But friend-ships are almost like living things. They grow and change. They need to be tended or they die. The way they start is not necessarily the way they will always be. Close, healthy friendships can survive changes—they may even thrive on it. But some-times, friendships end.

Close friends don't always stay that way, but the experiences—good and bad—from a friendship can often contribute to stronger relationships down the road.

The process may be gradual, as two friends develop other interests and friends. They grow apart as they find they do not want to spend as much time together. Or, something big might happen. A fight that isn't handled well, even if it's over something silly, may bring an end to a friendship. Other times, life gets in the way. When a person moves out of town or changes schools, it will probably mean she will get to see her old friends less often, if at all.

Sometimes, friends just drift apart. It's no one's fault; it's just the way it happens. Other times the feeling isn't mutual, and one person ends up feeling insulted or hurt when she gets "dumped." It's always painful to find out you're not wanted, and there's no easy way to get through this process. But there are strategies for getting through it. Sitting at home feeling sorry for yourself may be tempting, but it only gives you more time to obsess

WHEN YOUR PARENTS DON'T LIKE YOUR FRIENDS

Everyone doesn't like everybody. That's the nature of the world. But it can be a problem if your parents decide they don't like one of your friends or your group of friends in general. If this happens, try not to get immediately defensive. Remember, they're probably not just trying to give you a hard time. Listen to what they have to say. It's possible they've observed something in your friend's behavior that you missed. If you think they are wrong, calmly explain why. Ask if you can invite your friend to dinner or on another family outing where your parents will have a chance to get to know her better. If it's just a personality difference, try to explain to your parents that you want the chance to choose your own friends. However, if they are concerned about something more serious, you may need to take their advice and cool the friendship.

over what happened. A better approach is to get back to the business of living. Make a date to do something with another friend. If you can't face a social situation, don't just lie on your bed moping. Pick up a project that's been sitting in your closet for three months or start a new one. You may still feel sad—

that's natural—but involving yourself in other things will help you realize your world is not limited to one person.

Occasionally there are more important reasons to end a friendship—even if that wasn't what you wanted. If a girl treats you like an on-again, off-again friend,

Teens face all kinds of pressure, but true friends should never try to force one another to drink, smoke, take drugs, or engage in other dangerous behavior.

consider what her motives are in being your friend. Real friends don't use each other only when it's convenient. They don't betray you, make fun of you, or deliberately try to make you feel bad. "Frenemies" — people who say they are your friends but act more like your enemies—don't have your best interests at heart. Friends also should not pressure you to do something that is dangerous or makes you feel uncomfortable. That's a sign that it's probably time to say good-bye. If someone asks you to drink, do drugs, steal, vandalize, hassle other kids, or otherwise act in a way that's not cool, walk away. A friend can push you to try for the best in yourself, but she should never expect you to sink to the worst.

SMART AND SOCIAL

Today's teens have a lot going on. They're busier than ever before with school and activities. On top of that, their friendships require more managing due to electronic communication such as cell phones and texting and social networking sites like Facebook. It seems like everybody knows what everybody else is doing, all the time, which makes it even harder to deal with peer pressure or other problems within a friendship.

Always On

The number of ways to communicate has exploded over the last couple of decades, just in time for today's teens to take advantage of them. Cell phones are everywhere, and many middle schoolers have their own. Computers are now standard equipment in schools and most homes, giving kids

Girls: Being Best Friends

Keeping up via phone and the computer is fun—as long as private things are kept private. Don't share anything you wouldn't want a teacher or parent to see!

access to e-mail accounts, chat boards devoted to different groups, and social networking sites.

People can be available at any time, in an instant. Texting has made it easy for groups of friends to meet up without a lot of advance planning. With Facebook or similar sites, teens can update their status and all their friends can see it immediately.

Sure, it's fun to post a quick note about what's going on in your life, especially if it's something you want everyone to know. It's quicker than a phone call and more casual. People can respond if and when they want to. But this kind of communication has disadvantages, too. For example, many teens have hundreds of Facebook friends. It's impossible to sustain meaningful relationships with this many people. In addition, news spreads fast, and nowhere does it travel as fast

as it does on the Internet. Even if you don't post something online, something you tell a friend may end up on her page. This means that it's much more difficult to keep things private.

Online communication is both very immediate and very public—even though the people communicating with each other are not actually together. Typing something into a box is not the same as saying it to someone's face. Unfortunately, this distance can stifle people's instincts not to hurt someone else's feelings. Many of the same rules apply to texting. Although it's not as public as a social networking site, texts can still be saved and forwarded to other people. Even though the communication is electronic, e-mails, texts, and online posts and comments should still follow the same rules of courtesy and appropriateness. If it's not something you would feel comfortable saying to your

TAKING IT OFFLINE

Everyone knows when Paris Hilton has a fight with her best friend, but do you really want to be the star of the gossip mill? If you are angry with a friend, don't post the details online. It's between you and her, and hurtful comments that everyone can see will make it that much harder to make up later. Likewise, if you decide to "unfriend" someone on Facebook, don't make it a big deal. You can click a button to quietly remove her from your list—there's no need to make a big announcement. Everyone faces certain awkward situations in life, like breaking up with someone, whether it's a friend or a boyfriend. It's tempting to avoid the face-to-face awkwardness by simply sending a text or even changing your relationship status on Facebook. However, while that gets the message across, it's insensitive. Even when you've decided to move on, you should still break the news in private—and in person.

friend's face, then don't put it online or in a text.

Peer Pressure

It's great to have friends with whom you can do things, but what's not great is feeling like you have to do something you don't want to. Especially if you're part of a group of people, you can feel enormous pressure to do what everyone else is doing. Sometimes it's obvious that you should say no, such as if the people you're with are drinking or doing drugs. Other times, it's not so easy. For example,

Open communication is great, but sometimes sharing information degenerates into gossip and rumors, leaving the targets feeling isolated. It's usually best to steer clear of gossip.

maybe everyone is taking a turn at karaoke. There's nothing wrong with that, but if you just don't want to do it, you should be able to say no without feeling like you can't still be part of the group.

Bullying is another problem that girls face. A popular clique of girls—or even just one girl—can easily turn on someone who is less popular and more vulnerable. Bullies aren't necessarily bad people. They usually have insecurities

of their own. Often, they're trying to cover up the lack of control they feel they have over their own lives by taking it out on others. Sometimes they may not even realize what they're doing or how serious it is. They will just call it "teasing." However, bullying is extremely mean, and it can have serious consequences. If you feel like you are being bullied, you should speak up. And if you feel like you have to bully someone else in order

TURNING TO ADULTS

Part of growing up is learning how to deal with your own problems. However, part of dealing with your own problems is knowing when to get outside help. Sometimes a friend might bring up something that makes you feel uncomfortable. Maybe she has a problem that is too big for you to help her with. It's OK not to have all the answers. The most important thing is to listen. If it's a serious problem, however, you can advise her to seek out someone else's help—such as her parents or a teacher. If she's doing something that is dangerous or illegal, you should speak up even if she won't. She may be angry with you for a while, and it's even possible you'll lose her friendship permanently, but you will have done what a true friend should.

to stay with the "in crowd," it's not worth it.

If you're not sure whether someone is a bully or not, ask yourself these questions: Does the person always need to be in control? Is she constantly criticizing other people? Does she have the power to decide who's "in" or "out"? Are people afraid of what she will do if they don't agree with her or

follow her rules? The more "yes" answers you give, the more likely there is to be a problem.

Being Your Own Best Friend

Perhaps the most important key to making and keeping friends is to turn inward and look at yourself. Are you the kind of person you would want to be

Time alone helps people get to know themselves and helps prepare them to be a good friend. The best friend you can have is yourself!

friends with? If not, what changes would you like to make? Some friends last a lifetime, but not all do. Throughout your life, you will lose some friends and be challenged to make new ones. But there is one person you can stay friends with your entire life, no matter what: yourself.

Learning how to spend time by yourself may take a little practice if you're not used to it, but it's a great skill to have. You can keep yourself company if your other friends are busy or if you've had a falling out with someone. It's great to be interested in other people, but you don't want to have to cling to them because you have nothing else to do. Spending time alone also gives you valuable time to think about things without anyone contradicting you. Take the time to form your own opinions, and then you can see how others feel. No matter how many friends you have, it's important to develop your own interests and become your own person.

If you can accept and like yourself, then you will project the image of a girl who is confident and interesting. If you can learn to be nice to yourself, it will spill over into how you treat other people. It's important to be the person you would want to be friends with, but even more important is just being the person you want to be. That will bring you the best friends of all.

10 GREAT QUESTIONS TO ASK A GUIDANCE COUNSELOR

1. What's the best way to meet people?

2. What can I do to make people like me more?

3. How can I tell a friend that I don't want to hang out as much with her anymore?

4. My friends have started making plans and not including me, but they won't tell me why. What should I do?

5. My schedule and other commitments make it so I hardly ever see my friends, and I feel like I'm losing touch. What can I do about it?

6. What should I do if someone is always teasing me?

7. I have a friend who's doing things she shouldn't do, and I'm worried. How should I bring it up with her?

8. How can I tell my friend that I don't like how she's treating me, without making her angry?

9. My friend made me feel bad, and even though she apologized, I can't get over it. What should I do?

10. How can I stop feeling jealous of my friends?

MYTHS AND FACTS

Myth: It's important to have a lot in common with someone in order to be friends with her.
Fact: People who have different interests can be great friends. They can learn from each other and share their activities and knowledge.

Myth: The best way to maintain a friendship is to spend as much time together as possible.
Fact: Even good friends can feel smothered if they spend too much time together. Time apart lets people develop other friendships, pursue other activities, and come back with a new perspective.

Myth: If you have a problem with a friend, you should tell her exactly what she needs to do to fix things.
Fact: Problems aren't usually caused by only one person. In order to improve the relationship, both people usually need to make changes and look for compromises.

GLOSSARY

acknowledge To notice or recognize.

bicker To argue about unimportant things without reaching a resolution.

charismatic Having a personality that attracts people.

clique A close group of people who exclude outsiders and sometimes tease or bully them.

cultivate To nurture; to do things to make something grow.

evaluate To consider and come to a conclusion about the quality of something.

flaunt To show off; to attract too much attention.

frenemies A combination of "friend" and "enemy"; people who are supposedly friends but may do things that hurt the other.

gloat To show so much pride or happiness about something that it is hurtful or irritating to others.

inevitable Unavoidable; inescapable.

intimidating Having the ability to make someone feel frightened or uncertain.

ostracize To shut out or exclude someone from a society or group.

salvage To rescue; to find something good.

social networking site A Web site devoted to developing and maintaining friendships or other social activities.

stifle To smother or repress.

syndrome A disease or condition.

thrive To flourish.

toxic Dangerous or damaging; poisonous.

trait Characteristic.

vulnerable Likely to be hurt.

American Girl
8400 Fairway Place
Middleton, WI 53562
(608) 836-4848
Web site: http://www.americangirl.com
Books, dolls, and other merchandise explore the fictional lives
of several girls in various periods of American history. The
company's Web site offers interactive activities.

Camp Fire USA
1100 Walnut Street, Suite 1900
Kansas City, MO 64106-2197
(816) 285-2010
E-mail: info@campfireusa.org
Web site: http://www.campfireusa.org
Camp Fire USA offers programs to help children, both boys and girls,
develop their talents and interests, become empowered, and
contribute to society.

Girl Guides of Canada
50 Merton Street
Toronto, ON M4S 1A3
Canada
(416) 487-5281
Web site: http://www.girlguides.ca
Girl Guides of Canada encourages girls of all ages to participate
in activities that strengthen character and build community
relationships.

Girl Scouts of the USA
420 Fifth Avenue
New York, NY 10018-2798
(212) 852-2000
Web site: http://www.girlscouts.org
More than three million girls are members of this hundred-year-old
    organization, which builds girls' friendships and leadership skills
    through experiences that include sports, field trips, and community
    service projects.

Girls, Inc.
120 Wall Street
New York, NY 10005-3902
(800) 374-4475
E-mail: communications@girlsinc.org
Web site: http://www.girlsinc.org
Through various educational programs, this organization encourages
    and empowers girls to take part in their communities, build lead-
    ership skills, and develop their potential. An online site offers
    way to set goals and connect with other girls.

National Organization for Women (NOW)
1100 H Street NW, 3rd Floor
Washington, DC 20005
(202) 628-8669
Web site: http://www.now.org
Founded in 1966, NOW works for equality and women's rights in areas
    such as employment, schools, health care, and the justice system.

New Moon Girl Media
P.O. Box 161287
Duluth, MN 55816
Web site: http://www.newmoon.com
Through its flagship magazine and a Web site with information and
        activities, New Moon seeks to explore the various issues girls
        face and to connect them with each other.

This Is Me, Inc.
4315 North Richmond, #1S
Chicago, IL 60618
(773) 991-1194
Web site: http://www.thisismeinc.org
This group's variety of programs are focused on helping girls explore
        their interests and talents while under the mentorship of adult
        women.

Web Sites

Due to the changing nature of Internet links, Rosen Publishing has
developed an online list of Web sites related to the subject of this
book. This site is updated regularly. Please use this link to access
the list:

http://www.rosenlinks.com/r101/bff

FOR FURTHER READING

Bryant, Annie. *Worst Enemies/Best Friends* (Beacon Street Girls). New York, NY: Aladdin, 2008.

Burton, Bonnie. *Girls Against Girls: Why We Are Mean to Each Other and How We Can Change*. San Francisco, CA: Zest Books, 2009.

Carnegie, Donna Dale. *How to Win Friends and Influence People for Teen Girls*. New York, NY: Fireside, 2005.

Criswell, Patti Kelley. *A Smart Girl's Guide to Knowing What to Say*. Middleton, WI: American Girl Publishing, 2011.

Criswell, Patti Kelley, and Stacy Peterson. *Friends: Making Them and Keeping Them*. Middleton, WI: American Girl Publishing, 2006.

Dee, Catherine, ed. *The Girls' Book of Friends: Cool Quotes, True Stories, Secrets and More*. New York, NY: Little, Brown Books for Young Readers, 2008.

Harris, Ashley Rae. *Cliques, Crushes, and True Friends: Developing Healthy Relationships*. Edina, MN: ABDO Publishing, 2008.

Karres, Erika V. Shearin. *Mean Chicks, Cliques, and Dirty Tricks: A Real Girl's Guide to Getting Through the Day with Smarts and Style*. 2nd ed. Avon, MA: Adams Media, 2010.

King, Bart, and Jennifer Kalis. *The Big Book of Girl Stuff*. Layton, UT: Gibbs Smith, 2006.

Kitanidis, Phoebe. *Fab Girls Guide to Friendship Hardship*. San Jose, CA: Discovery Girls, 2007.

Lavinthal, Andrea, and Jessica Rozler. *Friend or Frenemy? A Guide to the Friends You Need and the Ones You Don't*. New York, NY: Harper Paperbacks, 2008.

Murphy, Pat. *The Wild Girls*. New York, NY: Viking Juvenile, 2007.

Myracle, Lauren. *Twelve*. New York, NY: Dutton Juvenile, 2007.

Mysko, Claire. *You're Amazing! A No-Pressure Guide to Being Your Best Self*. Avon, MA: Adams Media, 2008.

O'Sullivan, Joanne. *The Girls' World Book of Friendship Crafts: Cool Stuff to Make with Your Best Friends*. Asheville, NC: Lark Books, 2005.

Owens, L. L. *Frenemies: Dealing with Friend Drama*. Edina, MN: ABDO Publishing, 2010.

Reece, Gemma. *The Girls' Book of Friendship: How to Be the Best Friend Ever*. London, England: Buster Books, 2010.

Rinaldi, Ann. *An Unlikely Friendship: A Novel of Mary Todd Lincoln and Elizabeth Keckley*. New York, NY: Houghton Mifflin Harcourt, 2008.

Rushton, Rosie. *Friends, Enemies*. New York, NY: Hyperion, 2006.

Yee, Lisa. *So Totally Emily Ebers*. New York, NY: Arthur A. Levine Books, 2008.

BIBLIOGRAPHY

Annechild, Annette. *I Can Tell Her Anything: The Power of Girl Talk.* New York, NY: Marlowe and Company, 2005.

Apter, Terri, and Ruthellen Josselson. *Best Friends: The Pleasures and Perils of Girls' and Women's Friendships.* New York, NY: Crown Publishers, 1998.

Barash, Susan Shapiro. *Toxic Friends: The Antidote for Women Stuck in Complicated Friendships.* New York, NY: St. Martin's, 2010.

Besag, Valerie E. *Understanding Girls' Friendships, Fights and Feuds: A Practical Approach to Girls' Bullying.* Berkshire, England: Open University Press, 2006.

Bonior, Andrea. *The Friendship Fix: The Complete Guide to Choosing, Losing, and Keeping Up with Your Friends.* New York, NY: St. Martin's Griffin, 2011.

Brown, Lyn Mikel. *Girlfighting: Betrayal and Rejection Among Girls.* New York, NY: New York University Press, 2003.

Davis, Sarah Zacharias. *The Friends We Keep: A Woman's Quest for the Soul of Friendship.* Colorado Springs, CO: WaterBrook Press, 2009.

Dobransky, Paul. *The Power of Female Friendship: How Your Circle of Friends Shapes Your Life.* New York, NY: Plume, 2008.

Fields, Lisa. *Friends: How to Make, Keep, or Leave Them.* WebMD.com. Retrieved August 18, 2011 (http://teens.webmd.com/features/friendships-make-keep-leave-them).

Levine, Irene S. *Best Friends Forever: Surviving a Breakup with Your Best Friend.* New York, NY: Overlook Press, 2009.

PBS Parents. "Elementary School: When Friendship Hurts." PBS.org. Retrieved August 15, 2011 (http://www.pbs.org/parents/raisinggirls/friends/elem2.html).

PBS Parents. "The Laws of Friendship." PBS.org. Retrieved August 15, 2011 (http://www.pbs.org/parents/goingtoschool/social_friendship.html).

PBS Parents. "Understanding and Raising Girls: Middle School Survival." PBS.org. Retrieved August 15, 2011 (http://www.pbs.org/parents/raisinggirls/friends/mid1.html).

Wark, Penny. "Schools Must Take Account of Girls' Precarious Friendships." GuardianNews.com, March 22, 2011. Retrieved August 15, 2011 (http://www.guardian.co.uk/education/2011/mar/22/schools-beware-girls-friendships-precarious).

Wiseman, Rosalind. *Queen Bees and Wannabes: Helping Your Daughter Survive Cliques, Gossip, Boyfriends, and the New Realities of Girl World*. New York, NY: Three Rivers Press, 2009.

Yager, Jan. *Friendshifts: The Power of Friendship and How It Shapes Our Lives*. Stamford, CT: Hannacroix Creek Books, 1997.

INDEX

About the Author

Diane Bailey has written more than twenty nonfiction books for teens, on subjects ranging from sports to states to celebrities. She also writes fiction for kids and works as a freelance editor for other children's authors. Diane lives in Kansas with her two sons and two dogs.

Photo Credits

Cover, p. 1 iStockphoto.com/Jason Stitt; pp. 3, 20 (top) Compassionate Eye Foundation/Rennie Solis/Taxi/Getty Images; pp. 3, 26 (bottom) Wavebreak Media/Thinkstock; pp. 4–5 Ableimages/ Digital Vision/Getty Images; pp. 6, 14, 22, 29 iStockphoto.com/ Angelika Schwarz; pp. 7, 12 iStockphoto/Thinkstock; p. 9 © Grabowsky/ullstein bild/The Image Works; pp. 11, 23 Comstock/ Thinkstock; p. 15 Purestock/Getty Images; p. 17 iStockphoto.com/ Steve Debenport; p. 28 SW Productions/Photodisc/Getty Images; p. 30 Jupiterimages/Polka Dot/Getty Images; p. 33 iStockphoto .com/Christopher Futcher; p. 35 Francesco Carta fotografo/Flickr/ Getty Images; multiple interior background (orange) istockphoto.com/ stereohype.

Designer: Nicole Russo; Editor: Bethany Bryan;
Photo Researcher: Amy Feinberg